Manual

Factors of Adjustment and Satisfaction in Middle Adulthood Check List

Manual
Factors of Adjustment and Satisfaction in Middle Adulthood Check List

Dr. Shweta Nema

&

Prof. Indu Bansal

GenNext Publication

First Published, 2019

Published by

GenNext Publication
5, Ansari Road
Daryaganj, New Delhi-110002
Phone: 9811692060
E-mail: gennextpublication@hotmail.com

Printed at: G. Print Process, Delhi.

Cataloging in Publication Data—DK
Courtesy: D.K. Agencies (P) Ltd. <docinfo@dkagencies.com>

Nema, Shweta, author.
Manual factors of adjustment and satisfaction in middle adulthood check list / Dr. Shweta Nema & Prof. Indu Bansal.
pages cm
Study conducted in Narsimhapur District of Madhya Pradesh, India.
Includes bibliographical references.
ISBN 9789380223582

1. Middle-aged persons—India—Narsimhapur (District)—Psychology. 2. Married people—India—Narsimhapur (District)—Psychology. 3. Middle-aged persons—Health and hygiene—India—Narsimhapur (District) 4. Middle-aged persons—Family relationships—India—Narsimhapur (District) 5. Adjustment (Psychology)—India—Narsimhapur (District) 6. Satisfaction. I. Bansal, Indu, 1961- author. II. Title.

LCC HQ1059.5.I4N46 2019 | DDC 305.24409543 23

Introduction

In mid-age due to aging effect health start degrading, this not only affect their physical capabilities and economical productivity, but also cause significant psychological implications, like feeling of incapability, increased dependencies, depression. Expenses on medicines and chronic diseases increase financial burden which may cause sad and tense family environment, poor mental health and shattered peace. In this age due to overloaded burden from taking care of children and parent, adjusting family budget to fulfill needs of family members, they lack time for family, have little time to social life participation and getting along with others which may effect their social life satisfaction. Busy in making adjustments between family, social and professional responsibilities, mid-age couples tend to think too much which may cause feeling of low-satisfaction and unhappiness, peevish behavior, irritation and loose temperament, lack of focus or concentration, sad and feeling isolated. Being executive head of the family mid-age couples have to take decision on almost all family matters ranging from mundane household decisions to selecting colleges and making investments for better future. This requires a lot of energy and demands great responsibility.

Till mid-age, couples have faced numerous good and bad instances of married life together also develop a very good understanding of each other's behavior and attitude. Spouse becomes the best companion. However, there are many behavioral pattern of spouse which one does not like and accept. These patterns cause tensed family environment. Family becomes the binding force in relation between mid-aged couples. Family gives sense of togetherness and fulfillment in life but in many cases family become the major source of pain and unhappiness due to lack of cooperation and respect, stubborn nature of family members, children being in bad friendship, indifferent nature of family members.

Middle age couples are of vital importance in this age of changing social norms. Nema, S. Bansal, I. (2014) developed and standardized a Factors of Adjustment and Satisfaction in Middle Adulthood Check List in

Hindi to undue psychological stress and mental health problems. The tool was thus considered to be a diagnostic one. This could also be used as a research tool by the researchers who are investigating into the patterns of factors of adjustment and satisfaction. This was published under the caption Factors of Adjustment and Satisfaction in Middle Adulthood Check List in the year 2016. The main stages involved in the development and standardization of the check list were collection of items, pilot study, item analysis, reliability, validity and norms construction.

Method

The Factors of Adjustment and Satisfaction in Middle Adulthood Check List was developed on a sample of middle aged male and female population of Narsinghpur district (M.P.) ranging between 50-60 years of age. The method of sampling was purposively selected for the study. The size of the sample, however, differed from one step to another standardization procedure. The sampling scheme was as follows:

Item Analysis	Reliability	Validity	Norm Construction
N=555	N= 100	N= 100	N= 100

Pilot survey was conducted on middle aged couples to find out their perception on family factors of adjustment and life satisfaction. Researcher interviewed 50 middle age men and women (not included in final sample), between 50 to 60 years, to point out factors that contribute to their healthy adjustment from different groups and from different places. They were asked to give descriptive answers. To know the perception of middle aged people about various correlates of life satisfaction and marital adjustment, a questionnaire was developed in house. Although many environmental influences may decide adjustment pattern and life satisfaction of individuals but investigator concentrated on family factors of influence to pin point study and elicit in depth information of these factors.

Item Analysis

Based on what these people reported about problems and conflict in their life the researcher drew up a check list. This check list was further given to 2 psychologists, 2 sociologists and 5 Human Development professors in order to ensure the validity of the questionnaire. Finally investigator incorporated the suggestions of experts and finalized the questionnaire. Final form of inventory contains 81 statements categorized in five areas. Area wise number of items is given below:

Table 1

Areas	*No. of Items*
Physical illness and chronic disease	14
Mental health	16
Positive thinking and decision making	16
Relation with life partner	20
Family environment	15
Total	81

The items of different areas of adjustment and life satisfaction were also analyzed in items of inter correlations, to ascertain whether five areas selected to structure the check list were actually unrelated.

Table 2: Inter-Correlations Among different Areas of Adjustment and life satisfaction

	Physical illness and chronic disease	*Mental health*	*Positive thinking and decision making*	*Relation with life partner*	*Family environ-ment*
Physical illness and chronic disease		.732	.697	.563	.543
Mental health		—	.784	.602	.524
Positive thinking and decision making			—	.669	.534
Relation with life partner				—	.658
Family environment					—

The study of Table 2 indicates the inter-correlation among the five areas of adjustment and life satisfaction ranging from 0.524 to 0.784. While observing the inter-correlations between different areas of adjustment and life satisfaction one find that there exists a moderate correlation between some of them ('r' values at and above .6) whereas in more cases only it is between 0.524 to 0.563 (Mental health- Family environment, Family environment - Positive thinking and decision making, Family environment - Physical illness and chronic disease, Relation with life partner - Physical illness and chronic disease). The overall picture emerging out of this observation is that out of 10 inter-correlation values.

Reliability

After the items were analyzed, the next step adopted by the investigators, was to find out their reliability, in absence of which a psychometric tool carries little meaning. The reliability test used the Cronbanch's Alpha.

Table 3: Reliability

Cronbach's Alpha	*Cronbach's Alpha based on Standarized Items*	*No. of Items*
.893	.895	5

Validity

After reliability was found out, the step was taken up to assess the validity of the test which refers to whether the test measures that aspect of the measurement for which it has been constructed. The present test was validated on a sample of 555 couples (i.e. n=1110) cases by using the construct validation procedure.

Table 4: Inter-Item Correlation Matrix

	Physical illness and chronic disease	*Mental health*	*Positive thinking and decision making*	*Relation with life partner*	*Family environ-ment*
Physical illness and chronic disease	—	.732	.697	.563	.543
Mental health	.732	—	.784	.602	.524
Positive thinking and decision making	.697	.784	—	.669	.534
Relation with life partner	.563	.602	.669	—	.658
Family environment	.543	.524	.534	.658	—

Administration

Scoring

Respondent has to tick mark (√) statements which in their opinion lower their adjustment and life satisfactions. They are free to mark as many options as they find appropriate in their opinion. Area wise raw scores can also be obtained by adding all the Yes responses in each area category and can be used for further comparison of groups and statistical analysis with minimum score 0 for each area and maximum possible score as the number of items in that category.

Norms

After the test was validated, the percentile norms were developed because of their practicability and ease. Percentile scores represent the percentage of persons on the standardization sample, which fail below on a given raw score and provides a direct statement of individual's relative position in the standardization sample. The normative sample consisted of 336 male subjects who were in service and 197 male were in business and 22 male were retired from active service. 34 female subjects being in service and only 1 female subject being retire from service and 512 female subjects being house wives, were selected as sample for developing norms. In sort, the norms were developed separately for male and female subjects of the age group of 50 to 60 years of different categories.

References

1. Alder, E. S. (2010). *Age, education level, and length of courtship in relation to marital satisfaction* (Master's thesis, Pacific University, 2010). Retrieved from http://commons.pacificu.edu/spp/145
2. Anderson, T. B., McCulloch, B. J. (1993). Conjugal support: factor structure for older husbands and wives. *J Gerontol., 48*(3), 133-42.
3. Bookwala, J. (2005). The role of marital quality in physical health during the mature years. *Journal of Aging and Health, 17*(1), 85-104.
4. Berg, C. A., Schindler, I., Smith, T. W., Skinner, M., Beveridge, R. M. (2011). Perceptions of the cognitive compensation and interpersonal enjoyment functions of collaboration among middle-aged and older married couples. *Psychology and Aging, 26*(1), 167-173.
5. Carstensen, L. L., Gottman, J. M., Levenson, R. W. (1995). Emotional behavior in long-term marriage. *Psychology and Aging, 10*(1), 140-9.
6. Fielder, K. V., Kurpius, S. E. R. (2005). Marriage, stress and menopause: midlife challenges and joys. *Psicologia, 19*(1-2).
7. Gaunt, R. (2006). Couple similarity and marital satisfaction: are similar spouses happier? *J Pers., 74*(5), 1401-20.
8. Goel, S., Narang, D. K. (2012). Gender differences in marital adjustment, mental health and frustration reactions during middle age. *IOSR Journal of Humanities and Social Science,1*(3), 42-49.
9. Hashmi, H. A., Khurshid, M., Hassan, I. (2007). Marital adjustment, stress and depression among working and non-working married women. *Internet Journal of Medical Update, 2*(1).
10. Henry, N. J., Berg, C. A., Smith, T. W., & Florsheim, P. (2007). Positive and negative characteristics of marital interaction and their association with marital satisfaction in middle-aged and older couples. *Psychology and aging, 22*(3), 428-441.

11. Isaac, R., Shah, A. (2004). Sex roles and marital adjustment in Indian couples. *International Journal of Social Psychiatry, 50*(2), 129-41.

12. Jennifer, A. Volsky, Rushton (1998). *Intimacy, Marital Satisfaction, and Sexuality in Mature Couples.* (Thesis Concordia University Montréal, QuSbec, Canada) Retrieved from http://www.collectionscanada.gc.ca/obj/s4/f2/dsk2/tape15/PQDD_0003/MQ39448.pdf

13. Kashiwagi, K., Hirayama, J. (2003). Marital norm, reality and satisfaction in middle-aged couples: why are wives less satisfied than husbands? *Shinrigaku Kenkyu. [Article in Japanese], 74*(2), 122-30.

14. Lavalekar, A. (2007). Gender wise comparison on emotional intelligence and marital satisfaction. *Gender and Behaviour, 5*(2), 1388-1405.

15. Lee, J. E., Zarit, S. H., Rovine, M. J., Birditt, K. S., Fingerman, K. L. (2012). Middle-aged couples' exchanges of support with aging parents: patterns and association with marital satisfaction. *Gerontology. 58*(1), 88-96.

Factors of Adjustment and Satisfaction in Middle Adulthood Check List

नीचे विभिन्न स्थितियों से सम्बन्धित कुछ कथन दिये गये हैं उनको ध्यानपूर्वक पढ़ें तथा आपके विचार में इनमें से जो परिस्थितियाँ आपके समायोजन एवं संतुष्टि को प्रभावित करती हैं उन पर चिन्ह (√) लगाइये।

शारीरिक अस्वस्थता व लम्बी बीमारी :

1. दवाइयों पर अधिक खर्च
2. घर के अन्य सदस्यों पर निर्भरता बढ़ जाना
3. घर के सदस्यों का उपेक्षापूर्ण व्यवहार
4. अस्वस्थता में घर खर्च पूरा न कर पाना
5. अन्य सदस्यों की जरूरतों को पूरा न कर पाना
6. घटता हुआ शारीरिक सामर्थ्य
7. घर के कामों में हाथ न बंटा पाना
8. बार–बार दूसरों की सहायता की जरूरत
9. घर के सदस्यों का बात–बात पर शिकायत करना
10. घर वालों का आपको असहाय समझना
11. लगातार परहेज के कारण चटपटा व मसालेदार खाने की इच्छा
12. जीवन–साथी की व्यस्तता या बीमारी में अकेले सामाजिक जिम्मेदारी निभाना
13. परिवार के सदस्य में असाध्य बीमारी के कारण दिनचर्या में बदलाव
14. बीमार सदस्य की देखभाल की जिम्मेदारी होना

मानसिक स्वास्थ्य :

1. दैनिक जीवन के कार्यों में मन शांत न रख पाना
2. छोटी–छोटी परेशानियों को भी बढ़ा–चढ़ा कर देखना
3. गलतियाँ स्वीकार न कर पाना
4. परिवार को समय न दे पाने पर आत्मग्लानि होना
5. मतभेदों को हमेशा मन में पाले रखना
6. नीरस जीवन

7. पहले जैसा उत्साह न रहना
8. किसी भी मुद्दे पर अत्यधिक सोचते रहना
9. अत्यधिक चिन्ता
10. पहले की अपेक्षा अधिक गुस्सा
11. सदैव कुछ बुरा होने की आशंका
12. विचारों का मेल न खाना
13. झगड़ालू प्रवृति
14. सदैव नकारात्मक विचार आना
15. जीवन की निरर्थकता का अनुभव
16. चिड़चिड़ाहट / झुंझलाहट

सकारात्मक सोच एवं निर्णय क्षमता :

1. घर के सदस्यों का आपके निर्णयों को न मानना
2. अकेले निर्णय लेना
3. भावनाओं में बहकर जल्द निर्णय लेना
4. निर्णयों में सबको शामिल न करना
5. कठिनाइयों में संतुलित न रह पाना
6. आपके काम की प्रशंसा किसी और को मिलना
7. समस्याओं में खुद पर नियंत्रण न रख पाना
8. समस्याओं का समाधान न ढूंढ पाना
9. समस्याएं सुलझाने के लिए परिवार के सदस्यों पर निर्भरता
10. अपने गलत निर्णयों पर पछतावा
11. दूसरों के सुझावों को अहमियत न देना
12. अनिर्णय की स्थिति
13. दूसरों के निर्णय मानने की बाध्यता
14. अतीत के बारे में सोचते रहना
15. जीवन में जो नहीं मिला उसका अफसोस
16. दूसरों के कारण आपके साथ अन्याय की भावना

जीवन–साथी से सम्बन्ध :

1. जीवन–साथी का जिद्दी स्वभाव
2. जीवन–साथी का नकारात्मक होना
3. जीवन–साथी द्वारा बार–बार हीनता का अहसास कराना
4. जीवन–साथी का रोमांटिक न होना
5. जीवन–साथी के द्वारा अत्यधिक पाबंदी लगाई जाना

6. जीवन–साथी का आपकी गलतियाँ ढूढ़ना
7. जीवन–साथी के मित्रों का अक्सर घर आना
8. जीवन–साथी की तुलना दोस्तों या अन्य से करना
9. जीवन–साथी का शक करना
10. जीवन–साथी का कंजूस होना
11. जीवन–साथी द्वारा आपकी बुराई मित्रों व परिचितों से कहना
12. जीवन–साथी का आपके जैसा शैक्षिक स्तर का न होना
13. जीवन–साथी का फिजूल खर्च करना
14. जीवन–साथी का अत्यधिक महत्वाकांक्षी होना
15. जीवन–साथी का व्यसनों में लिप्त होना (तम्बाखू, बीड़ी, सिगरेट, शराब)
16. जीवन–साथी का आपसे उच्च पद पर होना
17. जीवन–साथी का अधिक वेतन पाना
18. जीवन–साथी का आपके परिवार के साथ व्यवहार अच्छा नहीं होना
19. जीवन–साथी का हिंसक व्यवहार/मारपीट
20. जीवन–साथी का हर बात पर बहस की आदत

परिवार का वातावरण :

1. कठोर अनुशासन
2. परिवार के सदस्यों में सहनशीलता न होना
3. परिवार में आदर–सम्मान न मिलना
4. बच्चों का आपसे दूर रहना
5. सदस्यों में अत्यधिक तर्क–विर्तक होना/अक्सर झगड़े होना
6. बच्चों की बुरी संगति
7. बच्चों पर अत्यधिक नियम कानून लगाना
8. बच्चों का देर रात तक बाहर रहना
9. बड़ी उम्र में भी बच्चों का आत्मनिर्भर न होना
10. बच्चों का आपके रहन–सहन व वेश–भूषा पर शर्म महसूस होना
11. परिवार के सदस्यों के मतों में भिन्नता
12. बच्चों का विद्रोही स्वभाव
13. परिवार के सदस्यों का विरोधी स्वभाव
14. परिवार में सबको मनमानी करने की छूट
15. परिवार के सदस्यों में आपसी सद्भाव की कमी